WEEKDAY CELE
FOR THE CHRISTIAN COMMUNITY

A RESOURCE BOOK
FOR DEACONS AND LAY MINISTERS

WEEKDAY CELEBRATIONS FOR THE CHRISTIAN COMMUNITY

A RESOURCE BOOK FOR DEACONS AND LAY MINISTERS

JOHN McCANN

VERITAS

Published 2000 by
Veritas Publications
7/8 Lower Abbey Street
Dublin 1

ISBN 1 85390 541 0

Designed by Bill Bolger
Printed in the Republic of Ireland by Betaprint Ltd, Dublin

FOREWORD

When, in 1988, the Congregation for Divine Worship issued the *Directory for Sunday Celebrations in the Absence of a Priest,* the fundamental point of the *Directory* was that the Christian celebration of Sunday should not be lost. This means remembering that the Mass remains the only proper way of celebrating Sunday. The aim of the *Directory* was to guide and to prescribe what should be done when circumstances require the decision to have Sunday celebrations in the absence of a priest.

The *Directory* reminds us that 'No Christian community is ever built up unless it has its roots and centre in the Eucharistic liturgy.' We are reminded also that the Eucharistic sacrifice cannot take place without a priest. The *Directory*, however, deals only with the Sunday Eucharist.

What, then, should be the approach to the community's need and desire for common worship on weekdays in the absence of a priest? In this book, Fr John McCann takes a sound theological and liturgical approach to the dilemma.

Too easily it is taken that a Holy Communion service is the answer. Unfortunately our practice in regard to receiving Holy Communion has not respected the integrity of the whole shape of the Eucharist. There is a difference between the celebration of the Eucharist and the reception of Holy Communion. There is a difference between a priest and a lay minister presiding over a Communion service. And there is a difference between pastoral and sacramental ministry.

In 1995, the bishops of Kansas issued a pastoral letter, *Sunday Communion Without Mass,* voicing their concerns about the 'blurring of these differences'. They state that they 'have come to judge that Holy Communion regularly received outside of Mass is a short-term solution that has all the makings of becoming a long-term problem'.

The community itself must come to a better understanding of liturgies other than that of the Eucharist. A better celebration of the Liturgy of the Word on Sundays would be a start. A more frequent communal celebration of the key hours of Morning and Evening Prayer would also help.

Much work of preparation will have to be done in training those who will preside at the community's prayer.

But above all, lay men and women will have to take their proper place in active participation at these acts of worship. This is part of that vision expressed by Pope John Paul II at an Audience in November 1998: 'Today, the Holy Spirit is spurring the Church to promote the vocation and mission of the lay faithful. Their participation and co-responsibility in the life of the Christian community and the many forms of their apostolate and service in society give us reason, at the dawn of the third millennium, to await with hope a mature and fruitful 'epiphany' of the laity. A similar expectation concerns the role that woman is called to assume. . . . These signs are closely connected to the abundant outpouring of the Holy Spirit, which the Church experienced in the preparation, celebration, and application of the Second Vatican Council.'

In this book, Fr McCann is giving a lead that will bear much fruit in the future.

Brian Magee CM
Veritas Liturgical Editor

INTRODUCTION

HOW TO USE THIS BOOK

There is a growing demand in Ireland for a resource book for weekday celebrations on those occasions when the celebration of Mass is not possible. This book is one response to that demand. The *easiest* way to use this book is simply to jump to the chapter that best seems to suit your needs; but this is not what I recommend. I believe it is important first of all to stand back from the issue and reflect: what seems most natural may not be the most beneficial in the long run. Hence I strongly suggest that you read Chapter One before you dip into any one of the proposed liturgies. Then you will be better equipped to make your choices.

CHAPTER ONE

DECIDING WHICH CELEBRATION IS MOST BENEFICIAL

The Need for a Daily Liturgy

While daily Mass is a feature of parish life everywhere in Ireland, it is becoming increasingly common to find that the celebration of Mass on every weekday is not always possible. By and large such situations are an exception, but they are likely to occur more frequently in the future. The need for a daily liturgy remains, whether it be Mass or not. The question arises as to what kind of liturgy might best be planned for such occasions. The answer is not at all obvious. A number of options are used around the world: Communion Service, Liturgy of the Word and Liturgy of the Hours. Many pastoral planners have, in practice, presumed that the obvious solution is a Communion Service, namely, a service that includes sharing in the eucharistic bread that has been consecrated at a previous celebration. This book provides also for two other alternatives: a simplified version of the Liturgy of the Hours and a Liturgy of the Word. The absence of an ordained priest presents an opportunity to develop these important ways of praying as a community. One might even go as far as to say that a parish community that is unable to worship in this way is liturgically malnourished. If people are only able or willing to gather for a service at which they receive Holy Communion, then we have fed them too narrow a version of what it means to be a worshipping community. Putting on Communion Services as a regular alternative to Mass may only compound this deficiency. It may be helpful to consider each type of celebration in turn before deciding which option is best in a particular parish or celebrating community.

Celebrating the Liturgy of the Hours

Although it has taken a variety of forms over the centuries, the Liturgy of the Hours has, from the earliest times, been considered the daily liturgy for the Christian people. With roots that go back to the Jewish liturgy and the practice of Jesus himself, it gradually took shape in the life of the early Church, and by the fourth century had become a popular gathering, frequented by the greater part of the community. Although various trends in the Middle Ages tended to confine its usage to the ordained and to those in religious life, the reform begun by Vatican II has encouraged its adoption once again as a liturgy for the whole People of God. Through this liturgy, all the baptised exercise their priesthood in a way that has an impact on all people, and contributes to the salvation of the whole world.[1] The promotion of the Liturgy of the Hours as a liturgy for common use has, nonetheless, been slow. The argument for promoting this daily liturgy was put strongly at a meeting of Italian liturgists back in the 1970s:

> It is well to recall that the priest would be fulfilling his responsibility only partially if he were to limit himself to nurturing only his personal devotion on the prayer of the hours and did not *try to bring the Christian people to share in it.* No step should be left untried toward restoring at least the more important hours, like morning prayer and evening prayer, to a place in the practice of the parish community, of youth groups, and of souls better trained in liturgical devotion; this is in fact being done with good results in many churches and communities.[2]

---

1   *General Instruction on the Liturgy of the Hours*, 7, 27.
2   Letter of Cardinal J. Villot to Bishop A. Mistrorigo, President of the Italian Bishops' Committee on Liturgy, on the occasion of the 21st National Liturgical Week of Italy, August 1970. English translation excerpt in International Commission on English in the Liturgy, *Documents on the Liturgy, 1963–1979: Conciliar, Papal, and Curial Texts* (Collegeville: The Liturgical Press, 1982), p. 157.

Those in our own country who have an appetite for daily liturgy are perhaps among the 'souls better trained in liturgical devotion' referred to above. A growing number of parishes in Ireland have already begun celebrating Morning Prayer before Mass, in order to cater for the needs of their weekday congregations. A key element in such a liturgy is the praying of psalms. Well-chosen psalms can give voice to the most personal dynamics of our lives and can provide true nourishment to the spirit.[3] Perhaps the occasional day without Mass presents an opportunity for this form of ecclesial prayer to grow, and for a fuller celebration of such a liturgy to develop. This kind of celebration can be a real experience of the presence of Christ; in the words of the Constitution on the Liturgy, 'He is present in his word since it is he himself who speaks when the holy scriptures are read in the Church' and 'he is present when the Church prays and sings, for he has promised "where two or three are gathered together in my name there am I in the midst of them"' (Matthew 18:20).[4] Most parishes that celebrate this daily office use *A Shorter Morning and Evening Prayer*, published by Collins. It is a modest volume, which could be bought in sufficient quantities for use by the smaller weekday congregation.

For those who have never celebrated the office before, the full office as given in the Roman Rite may be too complicated and daunting. In such a situation, a simple adaptation of Morning Prayer would perhaps be a good start. Chapter Two of this book gives such an adaptation. For evening services, a similar adaptation of Evening Prayer is proposed in Chapter Three. In each case, the suggested approach is to choose carefully a smaller number of texts, which people will come to know and love. Over time these can be complemented by other texts, so that the celebrating community

---

3   A few years ago a friend of mine was involved in a parish survey and found, to his surprise, that the most popular element in the Liturgy of the Word at Mass was the responsorial psalm. This may not be a universal phenomenon, but it does alert us to a possible pastoral opportunity.

4   *Sacrosanctum concilium* 7.

develops a larger 'repertoire' of texts to sing and pray. This is a stepping stone to praying the full text as given in the liturgical books. The celebration of Evening Prayer need not of course be confined to those evenings when there is no priest available for Mass. When well celebrated with music and a full use of the liturgical signs, a festive Evening Prayer can be a most attractive celebration, and suggests itself as an option to be considered on those special occasions when the parish wishes to gather for a festive liturgy. In this way, a larger group of people might also be given a taste for the Liturgy of the Hours.

In the historical development of the Liturgy of the Hours, two different forms or styles of celebration emerged. The first, sometimes referred to as the 'cathedral office', was a form that had immediate popular appeal, with plenty of music, well-known refrains, and lavish use of incense, movement and other liturgical signs. The other form, referred to often as the 'monastic office', was a more restrained, sober celebration that favoured a meditative contemplation of the scripture texts. Both styles have an appeal nowadays. Planners of celebrations of Morning Prayer or Evening Prayer might wish to consider which approach is most beneficial to the particular worshipping assembly; or they may decide to mix the styles somewhat, a practice adopted in the main in the current office as outlined in the Roman Rite.

Celebrating a Liturgy of the Word

In many parts of the world, a Liturgy of the Word is the celebration chosen when Mass is not possible, even on a Sunday. Recent Church documents underline the importance of appreciating the real presence of Christ in the proclamation of the scriptures.[5] Vatican II stated it eloquently:

---

5   Paul VI, *Mysterium Fidei*, 39.

The Church has always venerated the divine Scriptures as she venerated the Body of the Lord, in so far as she never ceases, particularly in the sacred liturgy, to partake of the bread of life and to offer it to the faithful from the one table of the Word of God and the Body of Christ.[6]

This is reminiscent of a striking statement of that great biblical scholar, St Jerome (d. 419–420):

For my own part, I think that the Gospel is the Body of Christ and that the Holy Scriptures are his teaching. When the Lord speaks of eating his flesh and of drinking his blood, this may certainly be understood as referring to the mystery [of the Eucharist]. However, the Word of the Scriptures and his teaching are [also] his true body and his true blood. [7]

St Jerome's reference to the Word of the Scriptures as the true body and true blood of Christ is arresting and may seem strange to us, but it does express forcefully the degree to which he venerated the scriptures. It speaks eloquently of a way of experiencing the presence of Christ when the eucharistic celebration is not possible. Vatican II also taught:

Sacred scripture is of the greatest importance in the celebration of the liturgy. . . . In order to achieve the restoration, progress, and adaptation of the sacred liturgy it is essential to promote that sweet and living love for sacred scripture to which the venerable tradition of Eastern and Western rites gives testimony.[8]

---

6   *Dei verbum*, 21.
7   *In isaiam Prologus. Corpus christianorum, Series latina*, vol. 63, 1. Cited in Lucien Deiss, *Celebration of the Word* (1991), English translation by Jane M. A. Burton (Collegeville: The Liturgical Press, 1993), p. 21.
8   *Sacrosanctum concilium* 24.

The importance of hearing the Word of God is also emphasised when the council speaks of the lay vocation: 'Only the light of faith and meditation on the Word of God can enable us to find everywhere and always the God "in whom we live and exist"' (Acts 17:28).[9] Within ecumenical dialogue too, the sacred Word is described as 'a precious instrument in the mighty hand of God for attaining to that unity which the Saviour holds out to all'.[10]

In our own country we have a long way to go when it comes to a deep appreciation of scripture as 'the bread of life'. Meditation on the scriptures is not as common as it might be, although the growth of interest in *lectio divina* is very encouraging. There is a growing awareness too in our country of the need for progress in the work of ecumenism. A veneration of the scriptures is something shared by all Christian denominations and offers a great opportunity for convergence. In the recent past, praying with scripture was commonly misunderstood as not being quite the 'Catholic thing to do'. Since Vatican II things have begun to change, but much more could be done. Perhaps the occasional absence of an ordained priest presents a pastoral opportunity to help people take more time with the scriptures and begin to appreciate the nourishment that they provide. There is a 'real presence' here to be discerned and 'tasted' in our parishes. A liturgy of this form will also heighten people's appreciation of the Liturgy of the Word as an important part of the Mass itself, and will thus enhance their eucharistic participation as well. It will also help us move towards unity among Christians at a local level.

What about Communion Services?

Another option that is proposed in some places is a Communion Service. This is a service in which people receive Eucharist that has

9 *Apostolicam actuositatem*, 4.
10 *Unitatis redintegratio*, 21.

been consecrated on a previous occasion and reserved in the tabernacle. It usually includes a Liturgy of the Word, often drawn from the weekday lectionary.

There is without doubt some precedent for a Communion Service outside Mass. In the early Church, especially in times of persecution, lay people regularly took the consecrated elements home to consume them on days when Eucharist was not celebrated. This practice did not last, however, and disappeared in the fourth century. The eastern liturgy has the Communion Service of the 'presanctified' on days when the Eucharist is not traditionally celebrated. The Roman Rite on the other hand has always been more cautious about such a rite. A Communion Service for the sick was developed in the Middle Ages, and, in 1600, priests were also permitted to hold Communion Services outside Mass for those who were not sick, although many local diocesan rituals discouraged this practice. There was, of course, the annual 'Mass of the presanctified', which formed the concluding part of the Celebration of the Lord's Passion on Good Friday. This only appeared in the Roman liturgy in the seventh century, and serious thought was given to its suppression in the reform of the rites after Vatican II.[11]

In 1973 the Sacred Congregation for Divine Worship issued a document entitled *Holy Communion and Worship of the Eucharist Outside Mass*. In this document the reception of communion during Mass itself is encouraged as the norm, but it also allows the giving of communion to those who request it for a legitimate reason outside Mass.[12] Special ministers of the Eucharist may also give communion when the priest is absent or impeded by sickness, old age or pastoral ministry. [13]

---

11 The reason for its retention was that communion for the faithful in this rite had only been reintroduced six years before the council, and it was felt that it was too soon to make a change.
12 Article 14.
13 Article 17.

There are, however, problems with this kind of service, particularly around its relationship with the Mass. Pastoral experience has shown that, in practice, many people who attend these services find it hard to distinguish them from the Mass, and yet such a service is very much a derivative celebration, which is incomplete when compared with the Mass itself. The eucharistic sharing that takes place in such a service has been detached from the organic whole to which it belongs — taking, blessing, breaking and sharing the elements in memory of Jesus. This ritual unity is stressed in the very document that permits Communion Services.[14] Many people do not even notice the absence of the taking, blessing and breaking of bread. This shows how little they have been helped to really participate in these essential elements of the Mass; to do without these aspects completely on a regular basis only compounds the difficulty. The difficulty here is that, in the Mass, our people still need to be educated into a sense of ownership of the eucharistic prayer. The elements are taken and blessed by the presider in the name of all the community. The eucharistic prayer, though proclaimed for the greater part by the priest, is a prayer that belongs to all. Further, the content of this blessing-thanksgiving prayer brings to the fore the sacrificial meaning of the sacred meal. Receiving communion in a rite that is detached from this aspect will tend, in practice, to empty it of much of its meaning. Similarly, the sign of the breaking of bread continues to be performed in such a minimal way in our celebration of Mass that the symbolism of unity in the breaking and sharing of one loaf is largely overlooked by participants. If they find in a Communion Service that this sign is entirely absent, their eucharistic sharing is all the more likely to be individualistic.

It can be argued that an occasional Communion Service is perhaps a good case of sensitivity to the devotional desires of parishioners, but if this becomes the normal experience (and there is every likelihood that in a few years' time this could happen, as it has elsewhere), our

14 Cf. Article 13.

lived theology of Eucharist will become skewed. Because people have for so long received pre-consecrated hosts from the tabernacle at Mass, it is not easy for them to perceive that their sharing in this food is a real participation in the sacrifice of Christ, made present at the altar. When this communion is completely detached from the Mass, the relationship between communion and sacrifice becomes still harder to perceive. In places where such services are regular, they are often called 'Mass' by participants, and are even preferred by many to 'the Mass that Father says', because they are shorter and often better prepared. A Communion Service may indeed be the short-term answer in some cases, but we need to take a good look at where it may lead in the long term, when an alternative to the Mass will be needed on a regular basis. The test is that such services should never become the normal or preferred experience of the Eucharist for participants; if this were to happen, it would indicate that our eucharistic practice is out of balance.

Chapter Five gives the necessary texts and indications for a Communion Service. Because there are a number of questions around the regular adoption of this kind of service, planners would do well to enquire as to any diocesan policy that might exist in this regard. In the Archdiocese of Dublin, for example, permission must be sought from the Archbishop before such services may be held.

CHAPTER TWO

A CELEBRATION OF MORNING PRAYER

Outline of the Celebration

- Opening Verse, 'O God, come to our aid . . .'
- Hymn
- Psalm, with Psalm Prayer
- The *Benedictus* canticle, sung or recited by all
- Intercessions
- The Lord's Prayer, sung or recited
- Concluding Prayer [1]

Introductory Notes

- This celebration is intended as a gentle introduction to the style of prayer found in the Liturgy of the Hours. The full celebration of Morning Prayer from the Liturgy of the Hours is preferable where feasible.
- The altar candles are lit for this celebration.
- The use of music will greatly enhance this celebration. Pieces can be chosen that do not need the support of choir or organist.

---

[1] Some of the prayer texts given here are taken from *Proclaiming All Your Wonders: Prayers for a Pilgrim People* (Dublin: Dominican Publications, 1991). This book contains a large variety of prayers for the Liturgy of the Hours as celebrated in the Cistercian tradition, and would be a valuable tool for use in the preparation of Liturgies of the Hours and Liturgies of the Word.

- All stand for the introductory verse. The sign of the cross is made while the verse is sung or recited.
- The hymn is sung.
- All sit for the psalm. This may be sung according to a psalm tone, or a psalm in responsorial style could be sung. A list of well-known responsorial psalms is given on page 45. It can also be recited in a number of different ways: (1) alternating between two groups, (2) alternating between the leader and the congregation, or (3) recited by a single person, while all listen.
- The psalm may be followed by a psalm prayer, recited by the leader. This is best preceded by a short moment of silence so that all can savour the meaning of the psalm just prayed.
- Being a Gospel text, the *Benedictus* is the high point of the celebration. All stand for the canticle. The sign of the cross is traditionally made at the beginning of this canticle. It is a good idea to sing it.
- The intercessions could be adapted or added to according to local needs.
- Some alternative psalms and concluding prayers are given at the end of this chapter.

Opening Verse
All stand.

Leader: O God, come to our aid.
All: O Lord, make haste to help us.
Glory be to the Father, and to the Son, and to the Holy Spirit,
as it was in the beginning, is now and ever shall be,
world without end. Amen. (Alleluia)
The Alleluia at the end of the doxology is omitted during Lent.

Hymn
All sing a suitable hymn, for example:

Christ be beside me, Christ be before me,
Christ be behind me, King of my heart.
Christ be within me, Christ be below me,
Christ be above me, never to part.

Christ on my right hand, Christ on my left hand,
Christ all around me, shield in the strife.
Christ in my sleeping, Christ in my sitting,
Christ in my rising, light of my life.

Christ be in all hearts thinking about me,
Christ be on all tongues telling of me.
Christ be the vision in eyes that see me,
In ears that hear me, Christ ever be.

Psalm
All sit.

Psalm 62 (63): 2–9

O God, you are my God, for you I long;
for you my soul is thirsting.
My body pines for you
like a dry, weary land without water.
So I gaze on you in the sanctuary
to see your strength and your glory.

For your love is better than life,
my lips will speak your praise.
So I will bless you all my life,
in your name I will lift up my hands.
My soul shall be filled as with a banquet,
my mouth shall praise you with joy.

On my bed I remember you,
On you I muse through the night
for you have been my help;
in the shadow of your wings I rejoice,
My soul clings to you;
your right hand holds me fast.

Glory be to the Father, and to the Son, and to the Holy Spirit,
as it was in the beginning, is now and ever shall be,
world without end. Amen.

After a brief moment of silent prayer, the leader may recite the following psalm prayer:

Leader: Father,
creator of unfailing light,
give that same light to those who call to you.
May our lips praise you;
our lives proclaim your goodness;
our work give you honour,
and our voices celebrate you for ever.

Through Christ our Lord.
All: Amen.

Gospel Canticle
All stand and sing or recite the canticle.

Blessed be the Lord, the God of Israel!
He has visited his people and redeemed them.

He has raised up for us a mighty saviour
in the house of David his servant,
as he promised by the lips of holy men,
those who were his prophets from of old.

A saviour who would free us from our foes,
from the hands of all who hate us.
So his love for our fathers is fulfilled
and his holy covenant remembered.

He swore to Abraham our father to grant us,
that free from fear, and saved from the hands of our foes,
we might serve him in holiness and justice
all the days of our life in his presence.

As for you, little child,
you shall be called a prophet of God, the Most High.
You shall go ahead of the Lord
to prepare his ways before him,

To make known to his people their salvation
through forgiveness of all their sins,
the loving kindness of the heart of our God
who visits us like the dawn from on high.

He will give light to those in darkness,
those who dwell in the shadow of death,
and guide us into the way of peace.

Glory be to the Father, and to the Son, and to the Holy Spirit,
as it was in the beginning, is now and ever shall be,
world without end. Amen.

The following version of the canticle may be sung to a simple tune
such as 'St Columba' (the same tune as 'The King of Love My
Shepherd Is') or 'Amazing Grace':

Now bless the God of Israel, who comes in love and pow'r,
Who raises from the royal house deliv'rance in this hour.

Through holy prophets God has sworn to free us from alarm,
To save us from the heavy hand of all who wish us harm.

Remembering the covenant, God rescues us from fear,
That we might serve in holiness and peace from year to year;

And you, my child, shall go before to preach, to prophesy,
That all may know the tender love, the grace of God most high.

In tender mercy, God will send the dayspring from on high,
Our rising sun, the light of life for those who sit and sigh.

God comes to guide our way to peace, that death shall reign no more,
Sing praises to the Holy One! O worship and adore!

Intercessions

Leader: Lord Jesus Christ, we thank you. Through your cross and resurrection you offer freedom and hope to those ready to receive them.
All: Lord, show us your loving kindness.

Leader: We are children of the day: help us to live in the light of your presence.
All: Lord, show us your loving kindness.

Leader: Guide our thoughts, our words, our actions: so that what we do today may be pleasing to you.
All: Lord, show us your loving kindness.

Leader: Help us to avoid wrongdoing: show us your mercy and love.
All: Lord, show us your loving kindness.

Leader: Through your passion and death you have won life for us: give us the strength of your Holy Spirit.
All: Lord, show us your loving kindness.

Other intercessions may be added, according to local need.

The Lord's Prayer

Leader: Let us pray with confidence to the Father, in the words our Saviour gave us.
All: Our Father...

Concluding Prayer

Leader: Lord, be the beginning and end
of all that we do and say.
Prompt our actions with your grace,
and complete them with your all-powerful help.
We make our prayer through our Lord Jesus Christ,
your Son, who lives and reigns with you and the Holy Spirit,
one God, for ever and ever.
All: Amen.

Conclusion of the Hour

Leader: The Lord bless us, and keep us from all evil, and bring us to everlasting life.
All: Amen.

Alternative Psalms for Use at Morning Prayer

Psalm 56 (57)

Have mercy on me, God, have mercy
for in you my soul has taken refuge.
In the shadow of your wings I take refuge
till the storms of destruction pass by.

I call to you God the Most High,
to you who have always been my help.
May you send from heaven and save me
and shame those who assail me.

O God, send your truth and your love.

My soul lies down among lions,
who would devour us, one and all.
Their teeth are spears and arrows,
their tongue a sharpened sword.

O God, arise above the heavens;
may your glory shine on earth!

They laid a snare for my steps,
my soul was bowed down.
They dug a pit in my path
but fell in it themselves.

My heart is ready, O God,
my heart is ready.
I will sing, I will sing your praise.
Awake my soul,
awake lyre and harp,
I will awake the dawn.

I will thank you Lord among the peoples,
among the nations I will praise you
for your love reaches to the heavens
and your truth to the skies.

O God, arise above the heavens;
may your glory shine on earth!

Glory be to the Father, and to the Son, and to the Holy Spirit,
as it was in the beginning, is now and ever shall be,
world without end. Amen.

Prayer

Leader: God of truth and love,
open our hearts to sing in praise
of Jesus your Son
whom you freed from the pit of death,
our risen saviour,
who is Lord for ever and ever.
All: Amen.

Psalm 150

Praise God in his holy place,
praise him in his mighty heavens.
Praise him for his powerful deeds,
praise his surpassing greatness.

O praise him with sound of trumpet,
praise him with lute and harp.
Praise him with timbrel and dance,
praise him with strings and pipes.

O praise him with resounding cymbals,
praise him with clashing of cymbals.
Let everything that lives and that breathes
give praise to the Lord.

Glory be to the Father, and to the Son, and to the Holy Spirit,
as it was in the beginning, is now and ever shall be,
world without end. Amen.

Prayer

Leader: Lord God,
maker of heaven and earth and of all created things,
you make your just ones holy
and you justify sinners who confess your name.
Hear us as we humbly pray to you:
give us eternal joy with your saints.
Through Christ our Lord.
All: Amen.

Psalm 50 (51)

This psalm would be particularly suitable for use during Lent.

Have mercy on me, God in your kindness.
In your compassion blot out my offence.
O wash me more and more from my guilt
and cleanse me from my sin.

My offences truly I know them;
my sin is always before me.
Against you, you alone, have I sinned;
what is evil in your sight I have done.

That you may be justified when you give sentence
and be without reproach when you judge,
O see, in guilt I was born,
a sinner was I conceived.

Indeed you love truth in the heart;
then in the secret of my heart teach me wisdom.
O purify me, then I shall be clean;
O wash me, I shall be whiter than snow.

Make me hear rejoicing and gladness,
that the bones you have crushed may revive.
From my sins turn away your face
and blot out all my guilt.

A pure heart create for me, God God,
put a steadfast spirit within me.
Do not cast me away from your presence,
nor deprive me of your holy spirit.

Give me again the joy of your help;
with a spirit of fervour sustain me,
that I may teach transgressors your ways
and sinners may return to you.

O rescue me, God, my helper,
and my tongue shall ring out your goodness.
O Lord, open my lips
and my mouth shall declare your praise.

For in sacrifice you take no delight,
burnt offering from me you would refuse,
my sacrifice, a contrite spirit.
A humbled, contrite heart you will not spurn.

In your goodness, show favour to Sion:
rebuild the walls of Jerusalem.
Then you will be pleased with lawful sacrifice,
holocausts offered on your altar.

Glory be to the Father, and to the Son, and to the Holy Spirit,
as it was in the beginning, is now and ever shall be,
world without end. Amen.

Prayer

Leader: Rescue us, Lord God, from the power of evil.
Receive the sinners who return to you
and renew our joy.
Open our lips
to proclaim your mighty deeds
and to sing the praises of him
who with his blood bought us at a great price,
your Son, who lives and reigns with you for ever and ever.

Alternative Concluding Prayers, for the Liturgical Seasons

Advent

Leader: Give us the grace, Lord,
to be ever on the watch for Christ, your Son.
When he comes and knocks at our door,
let him find us alert in prayer,
joyfully proclaiming his glory.
We make our prayer through our Lord Jesus Christ,
your Son, who lives and reigns with you and the Holy Spirit,
one God, for ever and ever.
All: Amen.

Christmas

Leader: God our Father,
by his coming on earth,
your Son revealed your glory to us.
May your Spirit awaken us to this radiance,
so that we may live in your presence through love,
straining forward to the day of eternity.
Hear us, through Jesus, your Son, our Lord.
All: Amen.

Lent

Leader: Turn our hearts to yourself, eternal Father,
so that, always seeking the one thing necessary
and devoting ourselves to works of charity,
we may worship you in spirit and in truth.
We make our prayer through our Lord Jesus Christ,
your Son, who lives and reigns with you and the Holy Spirit,
one God, for ever and ever.
All: Amen.

Easter

Leader: God of truth,
in the Resurrection of your Son
you reveal to us the meaning of all things.
Increase our faith
so that we may see your presence
in all that comes to us this day.
Hear us, through Jesus, the Christ, our Lord.
All: Amen.

Ordinary Time

Leader: Let the splendour of the Resurrection
light up our hearts and minds, Lord,
scattering the shadows of death,
and bringing us to the radiance of eternity.
We make our prayer through our Lord Jesus Christ,
your Son, who lives and reigns with you and the Holy Spirit,
one God, for ever and ever.
All: Amen.

CHAPTER THREE

A CELEBRATION OF EVENING PRAYER

Outline of the Celebration

- Opening Verse, 'O God, come to our aid . . .'
  or Lighting of an Evening Candle
- Hymn
- Psalm, with Psalm Prayer
- The *Magnificat* canticle, sung or recited by all
- Intercessions
- The Lord's Prayer, sung or recited
- Concluding Prayer

Introductory Notes

- This celebration is intended as a gentle introduction to the style of prayer found in the Litugy of the Hours. The full celebration of Evening Prayer from the Liturgy of the Hours is preferable where feasible.
- The altar candles are lit for this celebration.
- The use of music will greatly enhance this celebration. Pieces can be chosen that do not need the support of choir or organist.
- All stand for the introductory verse. The sign of the cross is made while the verse is sung or recited. Alternatively, a large candle could be lit, with the accompanying verse and response as given in the text. This brief service of light

continues the age-old custom that proclaims Christ as the light of the world as the darkness of evening begins to fall. There are various sung versions of the text in music collections such as *Worship, Gather, Ritual Song*[1] and *Celebration Hymnal for Everyone.*[2]

- The hymn is sung.
- All sit for the psalm. This may be sung according to a psalm tone, or a psalm in responsorial style could be sung. A list of well-known responsorial psalms is given on page 45. The psalm can also be recited in a number of different ways: (1) alternating between two groups, (2) alternating between the leader and the congregation, or (3) recited by a single person, while all listen.
- There is something to be said for using the same psalm again and again. People will become familiar with it and eventually know it off by heart. People might even be encouraged to pray the psalm at home on days when this celebration does not take place. Alternative psalms are also given. For a longer celebration, these could even be added in, rather than simply replacing the psalm given below.
- The psalm may be followed by a psalm prayer, recited by the leader. This is best preceded by a short moment of silence so that all can savour the meaning of the psalm just prayed.
- Being a Gospel text, the *Magnificat* is the high point of the celebration. All stand for the canticle. The sign of the cross is traditionally made at the beginning of this canticle. It is a good idea to sing it. Incense may be burned in a suitably prepared dish during this canticle.
- The intercessions could be adapted or added to according to local needs.

---

1   These are published by the Gregorian Institute of America (GIA Publications), Chicago.
2   Published by McCrimmons, Great Wakering.

- Some alternative hymns, psalms and concluding prayers are given at the end of the chapter.

Opening Verse
All stand.

Leader: O God, come to our aid.
All: O Lord, make haste to help us.
Glory be to the Father, and to the Son, and to the Holy Spirit,
As it was in the beginning, is now and ever shall be,
world without end. Amen. (Alleluia)
The Alleluia at the end of the doxology is omitted during Lent.

Alternative Opening to the Celebration
All stand. The one who leads the celebration lights a large evening candle and sings or says:

Leader: Light and peace in Jesus Christ our Lord.
All: Thanks be to God.

Hymn
All join in the following or another well-known hymn:

The day you gave us, Lord, is ended,
the darkness falls at your behest;
To you our morning hymns ascended,
your praise shall sanctify our rest.

We thank you that your Church, unsleeping
while earth rolls onward into light,
through all the world her watch is keeping,
and rests not now by day or night.

Across each continent and island
as dawn leads on another day,
the voice of pray'r is never silent,
nor dies the strain of praise away.

The sun that bids us rest is waking
your people 'neath the western sky,
and hour by hour new lips are making
your wondrous doings heard on high.

So be it Lord: your throne shall never,
like earth's proud empires, pass away;
your Kingdom stands, and grows for ever,
'till all your creatures own your sway.

If an evening candle has been lit at the beginning of the celebration, it may be incensed during the hymn.

Psalm
All sit.

Psalm 15 (16)

Preserve me, God, I take refuge in you.
I say to the Lord: 'You are my God.
My happiness lies in you alone'.

He has put into my heart a marvellous love
for the faithful ones who dwell in his land.
Those who choose other gods increase their sorrows.
Never will I offer their offerings of blood.
Never will I take their name upon my lips.

O Lord, it is you who are my portion and cup;
it is you yourself who are my prize.

The lot marked out for me is my delight:
welcome indeed the heritage that falls to me!

I will bless the Lord who gives me counsel,
who even at night directs my heart.
I keep the Lord ever in my sight:
since he is at my right hand, I shall stand firm.

And so my heart rejoices, my soul is glad;
even my body shall rest in safety.
For you will not leave my soul among the dead,
nor let your beloved know decay.

You will show me the path of life,
the fullness of joy in your presence,
at your right hand happiness for ever.

Glory be to the Father, and to the Son, and to the Holy Spirit,
as it was in the beginning, is now and ever shall be,
world without end. Amen.

Prayer

Leader: O God,
refuge of your people,
you did not leave your beloved Son among the dead
but raised him to your right hand.
Direct our hearts this evening,
that we may follow him on the path of life,
and find happiness in your presence for ever.

We ask this in the name of Jesus the Lord.
All: Amen.

Gospel Canticle

All stand and sing or recite the canticle. Incense may be burned in a suitably prepared bowl during the canticle.

My soul proclaims the greatness of the Lord,
my spirit rejoices in God my Saviour;
for he has looked with favour on his lowly servant,
and from this day all generations will call me blessed.

The Almighty has done great things for me:
holy is his Name.
He has mercy on those who fear him
in every generation.

He has shown the strength of his arm,
he has scattered the proud in their conceit.
He has cast down the mighty from their thrones,
and has lifted up the lowly.
He has filled the hungry with good things,
and has sent the rich away empty.

He has come to the help of his servant Israel
for he has remembered his promise of mercy,
the promise he made to our fathers,
to Abraham and his children for ever.

Glory be to the Father, and to the Son, and to the Holy Spirit,
as it was in the beginning, is now and ever shall be,
world without end. Amen.

The following version of the canticle can be sung to well-known tunes such as 'When I Survey the Wondrous Cross' and 'Come O Creator Spirit Blest':

My soul gives glory to the Lord,
In God my Saviour I rejoice.
My lowliness he did regard,
Exalting me by his own choice.

From this day all shall call me blest,
For he has done great things for me,
Of all great names his is the best,
For it is holy; strong is he.

His mercy goes to all who fear,
From age to age and to all parts.
His arm of strength to all is near;
He scatters those who have proud hearts.

He casts the mighty from their throne
And raises those of low degree;
He feeds the hungry as his own,
The rich depart in poverty.

He raised his servant Israel,
Rememb'ring his eternal grace,
As from of old he did foretell
To Abraham and all his race.

O Father, Son and Spirit blest,
In threefold name are you adored,
To you be ev'ry prayer addressed,
From age to age the only Lord.

Intercessions

Leader: Gathered together in faith and worship,
let us pray for our own needs
and for the whole human family.
All: Show us your loving kindness.

Leader: Renew your Church in our time, that together we may be a
sign of hope and reconciliation to all.
All: Show us your loving kindness.

Leader: Inspire and strengthen those in positions of authority, that
they may work for truthfulness, justice and peace.
All: Show us your loving kindness.

Leader: Hear the cry of the poor and suffering,
that they may find brothers and sisters who are generous and
compassionate.
All: Show us your loving kindness.

Leader: Lift up those who struggle with addictions and those in any
kind of trouble.
All: Show us your loving kindness.

Leader: Give rest and peace to all those who have died, and bring
comfort to those who mourn.
All: Show us your loving kindness.

Other intercessions may be added or substituted, according to local
need.

The Lord's Prayer

Leader: Let us pray with confidence to the Father, in the words our Saviour gave us.
All: Our Father…

Concluding Prayer

Leader: Father of our Lord Jesus Christ,
whose love never sleeps,
may the prayers of your people
rise before you this evening like sweet-smelling incense:
illumine our minds and our hearts
that even during the night hours
we may find joy in Christ,
the light of the world.

We ask this in the name of Jesus the Lord.
All: Amen.

Conclusion of the Hour

Leader: The Lord bless us, and keep us from all evil, and bring us to everlasting life.
All: Amen.

If desired, the celebration could conclude with a well-known Marian hymn such as 'When Creation Was Begun' or 'As I kneel Before You'.

Alternative Evening Hymns

O radiant Light, O Sun divine
Of God the Father's deathless face,
O image of the Light sublime
That fills the heav'nly dwelling place.

O Son of God, the source of life,
Praise is your due by night and day.
Our happy lips must raise the strain
Of your esteemed and splendid name.

Lord Jesus Christ, as daylight fades,
As shine the lights of eventide,
We praise the Father with the Son,
The Spirit blest, and with them one.

(This Hymn can be sung to the tune of 'All People that on Earth do
Dwell' and other melodies with the same metre)

Day is done, but love unfailing dwells ever here;
Shadows fall, but hope, prevailing, calms ev'ry fear.
God, our maker, none forsaking,
Take our hearts, of Love's own making,
Watch our sleeping, guard our waking,
Be always near.

Dark descends, but light unending shines through our night;
You are with us, ever lending new strength to sight:
One in love, your truth confessing,
One in hope of heaven's blessing,
May we see, in love's possessing,
Love's endless light!

Alternative Psalms for Evening Prayer

Psalm 138 (139): 1–18, 23–24

O Lord, you search me and you know me,
you know my resting and my rising,
you discern my purpose from afar.
You mark when I walk or lie down,
all my ways lie open to you.

Before ever a word is on my tongue
you know it, O Lord, through and through.
Behind and before you besiege me,
your hand ever laid upon me.
Too wonderful for me, this knowledge,
too high, beyond my reach.

O where can I go from your spirit,
or where can I flee from your face?
If I climb the heavens, you are there.
If I lie in the grave, you are there.

If I take the wings of the dawn
and dwell at the sea's furthest end,
even there your hand would lead me,
your right hand would hold me fast.

If I say 'Let the darkness hide me
and the light around me be night',
even darkness is not dark for you
and the night is as clear as the day.

For it was you who created my being,
knit me together in my mother's womb.
I thank you for the wonder of my being,
for the wonders of all your creation.

Already you knew my soul,
my body held no secret from you
when I was being fashioned in secret
and moulded in the depths of the earth.

Your eyes saw all my actions,
they were all of them written in your book;
every one of my days was decreed
before one of them came into being.

To me, how mysterious your thoughts,
the sum of the not to be numbered!
If I count them, they are more than the sand;
to finish, I must be eternal, like you.

O search me, God, and know my heart.
O test me and know my thoughts.
See that I follow not the wrong path
and lead me in the path of life eternal.

Glory be to the Father, and to the Son, and to the Holy Spirit,
as it was in the beginning, is now and ever shall be,
world without end. Amen.

Prayer

Leader: God our creator,
with incomparable wisdom you have fashioned us
in the image of your Son.
As the shadows deepen

illumine our hearts with the glory
that shines in the face of Christ,
that all our thoughts, words and actions
may speak of his ever-present love.

We ask this in the name of Jesus the Lord.
All: Amen.

Psalm 130 (131)

O Lord, my heart is not proud
nor haughty my eyes.
I have not gone after things too great
nor marvels beyond me.

Truly I have set my soul
in silence and peace.
As a child has rest in its mother's arms,
even so my soul.

O Israel, hope in the Lord
both now and for ever.

Glory be to the Father, and to the Son, and to the Holy Spirit,
as it was in the beginning, is now and ever shall be,
world without end. Amen.

Prayer

Leader: God of tender love,
who gave us Jesus, a meek and humble brother,
fill our hearts with trust and peace,
that we may follow him who is our Saviour,
and receive with joy
the kingdom promised to your children.

We ask this through Christ our Lord.
All: Amen.

Alternative Concluding Prayers

Advent

Leader: Almighty and ever-living God,
your strong yet gentle voice calls us
to prepare the way of Christ your Son.
Attune our spirits
to the workings of your love,
that we may welcome Jesus our Saviour
and experience the joy of the kingdom.

We ask this in the name of Jesus the Lord.
All: Amen.

Christmas

Leader: God, ever faithful and true,
whose love has come to dwell among us,
teach us the lessons of your Son's humble birth,
that amid the shadows and uncertainties of our lives,
his light may shine steadily in our hearts.

We ask this in the name of Jesus the Lord.
All: Amen.

Lent

Leader: Hear the prayers of your people, Lord,
who turn to you with all their hearts.
Renew within us

the spring of living water,
that we may prepare to celebrate with joy
the death and resurrection of Jesus
in whose blood we have been washed clean.

We ask this through Christ our Lord.
All: Amen.

Easter

Leader: Almighty God,
whose love is stronger than death.
Hear the prayers of your people,
as we thank you for the gifts of this day.
Guide and protect us this evening
that we may find peaceful rest
and rise again in joy to celebrate the victory of Jesus,
the bright Star of the Morning,

We ask this through Christ our Lord.
All: Amen.

CHAPTER FOUR

A LITURGY OF THE WORD

Outline of the Service

- Opening Song, during which the Lectionary is carried in procession to the ambo
- Lighting of candle(s) at the ambo
- Opening Prayer
- First Reading, followed by a short silence
- Responsorial Psalm, with a simple sung response
- Gospel Acclamation sung by all
- Gospel, followed by a short silence

} as in the weekday lectionary[1]

- As appropriate, a short reflection might be read from one of the many commentaries on the daily readings that are now available
- Intercessions
- Our Father
- Concluding Rite: The minister who leads the celebration concludes with a brief prayer. A simple *gesture* of reverence towards the scriptures could also be included. All present could, for example, kiss the book or make some other sign of reverence. A well-known hymn, suitable to the season, could also be sung.

---

1 On occasion, the praying community might decide to use readings other than those given in the weekday lectionary. For some suggestions, see p. 55ff.

Introductory Notes

- A well-known hymn is sung to begin the liturgy. Some examples are given below. While the hymn is sung, the lectionary is solemnly carried into the assembly and placed on the ambo.

- The importance of the scriptures could be further highlighted by lighting a candle or candles at the ambo. This could be done in silence, or with an appropriate verse and response.

- The readings and psalm are taken from the daily Mass lectionary or, as circumstances suggest, other readings may be substituted (see p. 55ff for examples).

- It is always advisable in liturgical celebrations to allow some silence between each of the scripture texts. This is all the more important in a liturgy such as this.

- The liturgy will be helped considerably if the responsorial psalm is sung. For this reason, it is quite in order to substitute the psalm of the day with another one that is better known. Even singing only the response, with verses recited, is preferable to a recited psalm. Some well-known settings are listed below.

- The gospel acclamation should always be sung, or else omitted.

- The Gospel is introduced simply with the words, 'Let us listen to the Holy Gospel according to N.'

- After a pause for reflection, a short reflective commentary on either of the passages might be read out. Examples of commentaries on weekday readings are listed below.

- Sample intercessions are given below. Use could be made of a variety of collections of prayers for weekdays. Sung responses such as 'Lord, hear our prayer' or 'O Lord, hear us we pray. O Lord, give us your love' could also be used to advantage. Space could also be allowed for spontaneous intercessions, according to the needs of the congregation.

Opening Song

The Lord's my shepherd, I'll not want.
He makes me down to lie
In pastures green, he leadeth me
The quiet waters by.

My soul he doth restore again,
And me to walk doth make
Within the paths of righteousness,
E'en for his own name's sake.

Yea, though I walk through death's dark vale,
Yet will I fear no ill;
For thou art with me, and thy rod
And staff me comfort still.

My table thou hast furnished
In presence of my foes:
My head thou dost with oil anoint,
And my cup overflows.

Goodness and mercy all my life
Shall surely follow me:
And in God's house for evermore
My dwelling-place shall be.

Procession with the Lectionary

During the opening song the Lectionary may be solemnly carried to
the ambo.

Lighting of Candle(s)

A candle or candles could be lit and placed near the place where the
word is to be proclaimed. The following verse and response could be
included:

Leader: Your word is a lamp for our steps.
All: And a light for our path.

Opening Prayer

Leader: We thank you and bless you, Lord our God.
In times past you spoke in many and varied ways through the prophets,
but in this, the final age, you have spoken through your Son
to reveal to all nations the riches of your grace.
May we who have met to ponder the scriptures
be filled with the knowledge of your will
in all wisdom and spiritual understanding,
and, pleasing you as we should in all things,
may we bear fruit in every good work.
We ask this through Christ our Lord.
All: Amen.

Alternative Opening Prayer for Advent

Leader: God of holiness,
you can make us strong by your grace
and vigilant by the power of your Gospel.
Sustain us in our striving at prayer,
and keep us faithful in meditating on your word,
that we may await with fervour
the coming of your Son, Jesus, our Lord.
All: Amen.

Alternative Opening Prayer for the Christmas Season

Leader: Loving Father,
your final word to us is your Word incarnate;
Grant that we may welcome him with all our hearts,
respond in love to your unending love,
and gain eternal life,

through Christ our Lord.
All: Amen.

Alternative Opening Prayer for Lent

Leader: Lord God,
your incarnate Word, Jesus Christ,
died because he remained faithful
to the message you had entrusted to him.
In this time of penance,
grant us the grace to love your word,
to ponder it in our hearts,
and allow it bear fruit within us,
for ever and ever.
All: Amen.

Alternative Opening Prayer for the Easter Season

Leader: Lord Jesus Christ,
you are the living word,
the power of the Resurrection.
Come and live in our hearts,
so that we may bear fruit for eternity,
you who reign with the Father,
for ever and ever.
All: Amen.

First Reading
This reading is taken from the daily Lectionary or, if circumstances suggest, from another source (see p. 55ff for suggestions).

Responsorial Psalm
The psalm is taken from the daily Lectionary, or a suitable musical setting is substituted. The following are among the better known examples from *Alleluia Amen*.

1. All the earth proclaim the Lord, sing your praise to God.

2. All you nations sing out your joy to the Lord, alleluia, alleluia.

3. May your love be upon us O Lord, as we place all our hope in you.

4. Molaigí an Tiarna, Alleluia.

5. My soul is longing for your peace, near to you my God.

6. The Lord is my shepherd, there is nothing I shall want.

7. Like the deer that yearns for running streams, so my soul is yearning for you, my God.

(Second Reading)
The second reading is read, if included in the lectionary.

Gospel Acclamation
All stand. The Gospel Acclamation is sung, or else omitted.

Gospel Reading
The Gospel is taken from the daily lectionary or, if circumstances suggest, from another source (see p. 55ff for suggestions).

Reflection
An appropriate reflection on the scriptures might be read.[2]

Intercessions and the Lord's Prayer
All stand for the intercessions. Various samples are given here.[3]

---

2   There are a number of published reflections on the readings of the daily lectionary. For some examples, see Appendix 2 of this chapter, on page 59.

3   A useful resource is *The Prayer of the Faithful for Weekdays,* edited by Eltin Griffin (Dublin: Dominican Publications, 1985).

For Ordinary Time

Leader: Gathered together in Christ
as brothers and sisters,
let us call to mind God's many blessings
and ask him to hear the prayers
which he himself inspires us to ask.

For our Pope N., our Bishop N., and all the Church's ministers
and the people they have been called to lead and serve,
we pray to the Lord:
All: Lord, hear our prayer.

For all those who serve us in public office
and for all those entrusted with the common good,
we pray to the Lord:
All: Lord, hear our prayer.

For all travellers, by land, air or sea;
for prisoners; and for those unjustly deprived of freedom,
we pray to the Lord:
All: Lord, hear our prayer.

For all of us gathered in this holy place
in faith, reverence and love of God,
we pray to the Lord:
All: Lord, hear our prayer.

Let us sum up our prayer and petitions in the words of Christ:
All: Our Father . . .

For the Season of Advent

Leader: My brothers and sisters,
as we prepare for the coming of our Lord Jesus Christ,

let us earnestly ask his mercy.
He came into the world
to preach the good news to the poor
and to heal the repentant sinner.
Let us ask him to come again to our world today,
bringing salvation to all who stand in need.

That the Lord Jesus may be with his Church
and guide it always,
we pray to the Lord:
All: Lord, have mercy.

That the Lord Jesus may bless the world with his peace
and the protection of his love,
we pray to the Lord:
All: Lord, have mercy.

That the Lord Jesus may heal the sick,
rid the world of hunger,
and protect us from all disasters,
we pray to the Lord:
All: Lord, have mercy.

That the Lord Jesus may find us
watching and ready at his coming,
we pray to the Lord:
All: Lord, have mercy.

Let us pray for the coming of the kingdom, as Jesus taught us:
All: Our Father . . .

For the Christmas Season

Leader: My brothers and sisters,
at this season,

the kindness and love of God our Saviour
has appeared among us.
Let us offer our prayers to God,
not trusting in our own good deeds,
but in his love for all humankind.

For the Church of God:
that we will joyfully proclaim and live our faith
in Christ the Word
who was born for us of the sinless Virgin Mary,
we pray to the Lord:
All: Lord, have mercy.

For the peace and well-being of the whole world:
that God's gifts to us in this life
will lead us to salvation in the life to come,
we pray to the Lord:
All: Lord, have mercy.

For those who suffer from hunger, sickness or loneliness:
that the mystery of Christ's birth
will bring them health and peace,
we pray to the Lord:
All: Lord, have mercy.

For our community and our families,
who welcome Christ into their lives:
that they learn to receive him
in the poor and suffering people of this world,
we pray to the Lord:
All: Lord, have mercy.

Following our Lord's teaching, let us say with faith and trust:
All: Our Father . . .

For the Season of Lent

Leader: My brothers and sisters,
we should pray at all times,
but especially during this season of Lent:
we should faithfully keep watch with Christ
and pray to our Father.

That Christians everywhere
may be responsive to the word of God
during this holy season,
we pray to the Lord:
All: Lord, have mercy.

That people everywhere may work for peace
to make these days the acceptable time
of God's help and salvation,
we pray to the Lord:
All: Lord, have mercy.

That all who have sinned or grown lukewarm
may turn to God again
during this time of reconciliation,
we pray to the Lord:
All: Lord, have mercy.

That we ourselves may learn to repent
and turn from sin
with all our hearts,
we pray to the Lord:
All: Lord, have mercy.

Let us now pray to the Father, in the words our Saviour gave us:
All: Our Father . . .

For the Easter Season

Leader: My brothers and sisters,
with joy at Christ's rising from the dead,
let us turn to God our Father in prayer.
He heard and answered the prayers
of the Son he loved so much;
let us trust that he will hear our petitions.

That pastors may lead in faith and serve in love
the flock entrusted to their care
by Christ the Good Shepherd,
we pray to the Lord:
All: Lord, hear our prayer.

That the whole world may rejoice in the blessing of true peace,
the peace Christ himself gives us,
we pray to the Lord:
All: Lord, hear our prayer.

That our suffering brothers and sisters
may have their sorrow turned into lasting joy,
we pray to the Lord:
All: Lord, hear our prayer.

That our community may have the faith and strength
to bear witness to Christ's resurrection,
we pray to the Lord:
All: Lord, hear our prayer.

Let us now together say those words which the Lord gave us as the
pattern of all prayer:
All: Our Father . . .

Concluding Rite

Leader: God, the Father of mercies, has sent his Son into the world.
Through the Holy Spirit, who will teach us all truth,
may he make us messengers of the Gospel
and witnesses of his love to the world.
All: Amen.

If desired, all present could make some personal gesture of reverence
towards the scriptures, for example, by kissing the book.

A well-known hymn could conclude the celebration. The following
are possible examples, suitable to each season:

Ordinary Time

Holy God we praise thy name.
Lord of all we bow before thee.
All on earth thy sceptre own.
All in heaven above adore thee.
Endless is thy vast domain.
Everlasting is thy reign.

Hark, with loud and pealing hymn,
Thee the angel choirs are praising;
Cherubim and seraphim,
One unceasing chorus raising,
Ever sing with sweet accord,
Holy, holy, holy Lord.

Advent

O come, O come, Emmanuel,
To free your captive Israel,

That mourns in lonely exile here,
Until the Son of God appear.

Rejoice, rejoice, O Israel,
To you shall come Emmanuel.

O royal branch of Jesse's tree,
Redeem us all from tyranny;
From pain of hell your people free,
And over death win victory.

Christmas

Angels we have heard on high,
Sweetly singing o'er the plains,
And the mountains in reply
Echo still their joyous strains:

Gloria in excelsis Deo;
Gloria in excelsis Deo.

Shepherds, why this jubilee?
Why your rapturous strain prolong?
Say what may your tidings be,
Which inspire your heavenly song.

Come to Bethlehem and see
Him whose birth the angels sing:
Come, adore on bended knee
Christ our Lord, the new-born king.

Lent
(Tune: The Old Hundredth)[4]

The glory of these forty days
We celebrate with songs of praise;
For Christ, by whom all things were made,
Himself has fasted and has prayed.

Alone and fasting, Moses saw
The loving God who gave the law;
And to Elijah, fasting, came
The steeds and chariots of flame.

So Daniel trained his mystic sight,
Delivered from the lion's might;
And John, the Bridegroom's friend, became
The herald of Messiah's name.

Then grant that we like them be true,
Consumed in fast and prayer with you;
Our spirits strengthen with your grace,
And give us joy to see your face.

---

4   This is the tune that is used for hymns such as 'All People that on Earth do
     Dwell' and 'Receive O Father in Thy Love'.

ADDITIONAL READINGS

When it comes to the choice of scripture readings for prayer services there is always the danger that we pick only those passages that we like to hear and avoid those that challenge or disturb. We can end up with a very selective reading of the Bible. One of the advantages of following the weekday lectionary is that it ensures that we hear all the more important passages of the Bible. It may happen however that a particular passage may prove difficult for a particular congregation to understand or not speak to their immediate context. Other readings might well be used on such occasions. Volume 3 of the Lectionary provides a substantial, ready-made selection of texts according to various themes. Some texts are listed below by way of example. One might also have recourse to other collections of scripture passages. The bottom line is that people actually hear the word of God!

Sample Texts from Volume 3 of the Lectionary[1]

The Word of God

Deut 6:3–9 *Let these words be written on your heart.* (p. 326)
Deut 30:10–14 *The word is very near to you for your observance.* (p. 327)
Is 55:10–11 *The word from my mouth does not return to me empty.* (p. 328)
Heb 4:12–13 *The word of God can judge secret emotions and thoughts.* (p. 321)
Lk 4:16–21 *This text is being fulfilled today even as you listen.* (p. 324)
Lk 24:44–48 *Everything written about me in the Law of Moses, in the Prophets and in the Psalms, has to be fulfilled.* (p. 334)

---

1   Page numbers from the 1981 edition for England and Wales, Scotland, Ireland.

The Love of Christ

Ex 34:4–6. 8–9. *Lord, Lord, a God of tenderness and compassion.* (p. 818)
Is 49:13–15 *Does a woman forget her baby! I will never forget you.* (p. 821)
Rom 8:31–35. 37–39 *Nothing can come between us and the love of Christ.* (p. 224)
Eph 3:14–19 *To know the love of Christ, which is beyond all knowledge.* (p. 830)
Jn 10:11–18 *The good shepherd is one who lays down his life for his sheep.* (p. 835)
Jn 15:9–17 *Remain in my love.* (p. 837)

The Holy Spirit

Is 61:1–3. 6. 8–9 *The spirit of the Lord has been given to me.* (p. 88)
Joel 3:1–5 *I will pour out my Spirit on all.* (p. 90)
Acts 2:1–6. 14. 22–23. 32–33 *They were all filled with the Holy Spirit, and began to speak.* (p. 93)
Rom 8:26–27 *The Spirit comes to help us in our weakness.* (p. 98)
1 Cor 12:4–13 *The gifts of the Spirit given for the good of all.* (p. 98)
Gal 5:16–17. 22–25 *Since the Spirit is our life, let us be directed by the Spirit.* (p. 99)
Jn 7:37–39 *Fountains of living water shall flow.* (p. 106)
Jn 14:23–26 *The Holy Spirit will teach you everything.* (p. 107)

Sin and Forgiveness

Joel 2:12–18 *Let your hearts be broken, not your garments torn.* (p. 703)
Mt 9:1–8 *Courage, my child, your sins are forgiven.* (p. 710)
Lk 15:1–3. 11–32 *The prodigal son.* (p. 713)

Healing

Is 61:1–3 *The Spirit of the Lord has sent me to comfort all those who mourn.* (p. 216)
Jas 5:13–16 *The prayer of faith shall save the sick.* (p. 673)

Mt 8:1–4 *If you want to, you can cure me.* (P. 233)
Mt 8:14–17 *He took our sicknesses away.* (p. 673)

Ministry and Service

1 Cor 12:3–7. 12–13 *There is a variety of gifts but always the same Spirit.* (p. 450)
Eph 4:1–7. 11–13. *The work of service, building up the body of Christ.* (p. 451)
Mt 20:20–28 *The Son of Man came not to be served but to serve.* (p. 455)
Jn 13:1–5 *Jesus washes the feet of his disciples.* (p. 5)
Lk 22:24–30 *I am among you as one who serves.* (p. 591)

The Mission of All God's People

Joel 3:1–5 *I will pour out my Spirit on all.* (p. 494)
1 Cor 12:3–7. 12–13 *There is a variety of gifts but always the same Spirit.* (p. 450)
1 Pet 2:4–10 *A chosen race, a royal priesthood, a consecrated nation.* (p. 499)
Mt 15:14–30 *The parable of the talents.* (p. 504)
Mk 3:31–35 *Anyone who does the will of God, that person is my brother and sister and mother.* (p. 505)

Unity among Christians

Eph 4:1–6 *Do all you can to preserve the unity of the Spirit by the peace that binds you together.* (p. 514)
Phil 2:1–13 *Being united, and being humble as Christ was humble.* (p. 514)
Col 3:9–17 *You were called together as parts of one body.* (p. 515)
Mt 18:19–22 *You must forgive seventy-seven times.* (p. 521)
Lk 9:59–56 *Anyone who is not against you is for you.* (p. 521)
Jn 17:20–26 *May they be so completely one.* (p. 527)

Justice and Peace

Num 6:22–27 *May the Lord uncover his face to you and bring you peace.* (p. 564)
Is 9:1–6 *Wide is his dominion in a peace that has no end.* (p. 593)

Is 32:15–18 *Integrity will bring peace.* (p. 568)
Is 58:6–11 *Share your bread with the hungry.* (p. 569)
Col 3:12–15 *May the peace of Christ reign in your hearts.* (p. 597)
Jas 3:13–18 *The work of peacemakers.* (p. 577)
Jas 4:1–10 *Conflict begins within ourselves.* (p. 577)
Mt 5:1–12 *Blessed are the peacemakers.* (p. 583)
Mt 5:38–48 *Love your enemies.* (p. 601)

Responding to Those in Special Need

Job 31:16–20. 24–25. 31–32. *Have I taken my share of bread alone, not giving a share to the orphan?* (p. 649)
Acts 11:27–30 *Relief to the famine in Judaea.* (p. 572)
2 Cor 8:1–5. 9–15 *It is a question of balancing your surplus now against their present need.* (p. 573)
2 Cor 9:6–15 *God loves a cheerful giver.* (p. 574)
Mt 25:31–46 *You did it to me.* (p. 587)
Lk 16:19–31 *There was a poor man, called Lazarus.* (p. 590)

Refugees and Exiles

Deut 10:17–19 *God loves the stranger.* (p. 659)
Deut 24:17–22 *Let anything left be for the stranger.* (p. 660)
Rom 12:9–16 *You should make hospitality your special care.* (p. 661)
Mt 2:13–15. 19–23 *Take the child and his mother and escape into Egypt.* (p. 664)
Lk 10:25–37 *Who is my neighbour?* (p. 666)

The Lord's Prayer

Hos 11:1. 3–4. 8–9 *I led them with leading-strings of love.* (p. 10)
Rom 8:14–17. 26–27 *The Spirit makes us cry out, 'Abba, Father!'* (p. 12)
Mt 6:9–13 *Say this when you pray.* (p. 13)

APPENDIX TWO TO CHAPTER FOUR

RESOURCES FOR REFLECTIONS ON THE READINGS OF THE WEEKDAY LECTIONARY

Bastin, Marcel (et al.). *God Day by Day: A Companion to the Weekday Missal,* London: Geoffrey Chapman, 1985. 5 Volumes.

Bible Alive. Monthly publication. Stoke-on-Trent: Graphic House (Outlet in Ireland: PO Box 10, Navan, Co. Meath).

Donders, Joseph G. *With Hearts on Fire: Reflections on the Weekday Readings of the Liturgical Year*. Mystic: Twenty-Third Publications, 1999.

Irwin, Kevin W. *Lent: A Guide to the Eucharist and Hours*, 1985
    Easter: A Guide to the Eucharist and Hours, 1991
New York: Pueblo Publishing Company

McKarns, James. *Give Us This Day: Reflections for Each Day of the Liturgical Year*. New York: Alba House, 1991.

Miller, Charles E., C.M. *Opening the Treasures: A Book of Daily Homily-Meditations*. New York: Alba House, 1982.

Scripture in Church. Dublin: Dominican Publications. Quarterly Publication.

Stuhlmueller, Carroll, C.P. *Biblical Meditations for Lent*
Biblical Meditations for the Easter Season
Biblical Meditations for Advent and the Christmas Season
Biblical Meditations for Ordinary Time (Weeks 1-9)
Biblical Meditations for Ordinary Time (Weeks 10-22)
Biblical Meditations for Ordinary Time (Weeks 23-34)
New York/Ramsey: Paulist Press

Romb, Anselm W. *Walk With the Lord*. Boston: St Paul's Books &
Media. 1990

The Weekday Living Word. Chawton: Redemptorist Publications. A bi-
monthly publication.

CHAPTER FIVE

A COMMUNION SERVICE

Preliminaries

1. Such a celebration ideally involves a number of ministers: a leader, a reader, eucharistic ministers and a music minister.
2. The celebration is led by a eucharistic minister who has been suitably prepared to lead public prayer.
3. In order to lessen any confusion between this service and the Mass, ministers should avoid any distinctive vesture, they should avoid using the presidential chair and they should only stand at the altar when the Blessed Sacrament is brought to it.

Outline of the Service

- Opening Song
- Sign of the Cross
- Penitential Rite
- Liturgy of the Word: Reading, Psalm, Gospel Acclamation, Gospel, Intercessions
- A minister of communion brings the Sacrament to the altar from the place where it is reserved. The leader goes to the altar and genuflects.
- The Lord's Prayer
- The leader invites all present to exchange a sign of peace.
- The leader takes some of the consecrated bread and shows it to the people with the usual invitation, 'This is the Lamb of God . . .'

- Communion takes place in the usual way, and may be accompanied by a suitable song.
- Silence, Psalm or Song of Praise
- Concluding Prayer
- Blessing: The leader signs himself or herself with the cross and says the blessing.
- Dismissal

Note for the Archdiocese of Dublin

Liturgical planners are asked to seek permission from the Archbishop before arranging the celebration of a Communion Service.

Introductory Rites

Opening Song

All stand. The service may begin with a suitable song, for example:

Christ be beside me, Christ be before me,
Christ be behind me, King of my heart.
Christ be within me, Christ be below me,
Christ be above me, never to part.

Christ on my right hand, Christ on my left hand,
Christ all around me, shield in the strife.
Christ in my sleeping, Christ in my sitting,
Christ in my rising, light of my life.

Christ be in all hearts thinking about me,
Christ be on all tongues telling of me.
Christ be the vision in eyes that see me,
In ears that hear me, Christ ever be.

Greeting
All remain standing as the minister says:
In the name of the Father, and of the Son, and of the Holy Spirit.
All: Amen.

The minister greets all present:
The grace and peace of God our Father and the Lord Jesus Christ be
with you.
All: And also with you.

Introduction
The minister introduces the celebration in these or similar words:

Once again we gather to be the Church of Christ.
Christ is with us, as he promised:
present in this assembly of his people,
in the proclamation of God's word,
and in the communion of his body and blood.

As our priest cannot be with us
we are unable to celebrate the Eucharist.
Let us reflect on the word and pray together
and then share Christ's body and blood
consecrated for us at a previous Eucharist.

Penitential Rite

Minister: Gathered together in Christ,
let us ask for forgiveness with confidence,
for God is full of gentleness and compassion.

A pause for silent reflection follows.

All: I confess to almighty God
and to you, my brothers and sisters,

that I have sinned through my own fault
in my thoughts and in my words,
in what I have done,
and in what I have failed to do;
and I ask blessed Mary, ever virgin,
all the angels and saints,
and you, my brothers and sisters,
to pray for me to the Lord our God.

Leader: May almighty God have mercy on us,
forgive us our sins,
and bring us to everlasting life.
All: Amen.

Celebration of the Word of God

The Liturgy of the Word now takes place, using the texts of the daily lectionary.

Reading

The scripture is proclaimed by a reader. A brief silence is observed.

Psalm

The responsorial psalm is sung or recited. See page 45 for well-known musical settings of responsorial psalms.

Gospel Acclamation

All stand. The gospal acclamation is either sung or omitted.

Gospel

The reader introduces the Gospel with the words, 'A Reading from the Holy Gospel according to N.'
A brief silence is observed after the proclamation of the Gospel.

General Intercessions

The liturgy of the word concludes with the General Intercessions, following the same format as at Mass.

Holy Communion
A eucharistic minister brings the Sacrament to the altar, from the place where it is reserved.

The Lord's Prayer
The leader introduces the Lord's Prayer in these or similar words:
Let us pray with confidence to the Father in the words our Saviour gave us.
All: Our Father . . .

Sign of Peace
The leader may invite the people to exchange the sign of peace, in these or similar words:
Let us offer each other the sign of peace.

Invitation to Communion
The leader genuflects. Taking the host, the leader raises the host slightly over the vessel or pyx and, facing the people, says:
This is the Lamb of God
who takes away the sins of the world.
Happy are those who are called to his supper.

All: Lord, I am not worthy to receive you,
but only say the word and I shall be healed.

Communion
If the leader receives communion, he or she says quietly,
May the body of Christ bring me to everlasting life.

Eucharistic ministers go to the communicants. They take a host for each one, raise it slightly and say:
The body of Christ.

The communicant receives communion, answering:
Amen.

Communion Song

During the distribution of communion, a hymn may be sung, for example:

Soul of my Saviour, sanctify my breast;
Body of Christ, be though my saving guest;
Blood of my Saviour, bathe me in thy tide,
Wash me, ye waters, streaming from his side.

Strength and protection may his passion be:
O blessed Jesus, hear and answer me:
Deep in thy wounds, Lord, hide and shelter me,
So shall I never, never part from thee.

Guard and defend me from the foe malign:
In death's dread moments make me only thine:
Call me, and bid me come to thee on high,
When I may praise thee with they saints for aye.

Silence, Psalm, or Song of Praise

A period of silence may now be observed, or a psalm or song of praise may be sung, for example:

Now thank we all our God
With hearts and hands and voices,
Who wondrous things has done,
In whom his world rejoices;
Who, from our mothers' arms,
Hath blest us on our way
With countless gifts of love,
And still is ours today.

All praise and thanks to God
The Father now be given,
The Son, and Spirit blest,

Who reigns in highest heaven,
Eternal, Triune God,
Whom earth and heav'n adore;
For thus it was, is now,
And shall be evermore.

Concluding Prayer
The leader then says one of the following concluding prayers:

Lord,
you have nourished us with one bread from heaven.
Fill us with your Spirit,
and make us one in peace and love.

We ask this through Christ our Lord.
All: Amen.

Or

Lord,
you renew us at your table with the bread of life.
May this food strengthen us in love
and help us to serve you in each other.

We ask this in the name of Jesus the Lord.
All: Amen.

Or

Lord,
we thank you for the nourishment you give us
through your holy gift.
Pour out your Spirit upon us
and in the strength of this food from heaven
keep us singleminded in your service.

We ask this in the name of Jesus the Lord.
All: Amen.

Concluding Rite

Blessing
The leader invokes God's blessing and, crossing himself or herself, says:

May the almighty and merciful God bless and protect us,
the Father, and the Son, + and the Holy Spirit.
All: Amen.

Dismissal

Leader: Go in the peace of Christ.
All: Thanks be to God.

ACKNOWLEDGEMENTS

Psalm 56 (57) from *The Grail Psalms: An Inclusive Language Version* (The Grail, 1986) is used by permission of The Grail (England).

Excerpts from *The Divine Office* (Vols. I & II), published in 1974 by Collins, E. J. Dwyer and Talbot, are reprinted with the permission of A. P. Watt Ltd on behalf of The Hierarchies of England and Wales, Ireland and Australia.

Excerpts from the English translation of *The Roman Missal* © 1973, International Committee on English in the Liturgy, Inc. (ICEL); excerpts from the English translation of *Holy Communion and Worship of the Eucharist outside Mass* © 1974, ICEL; excerpts from the English translation of *Documents on the Liturgy; 1963–1979: Conciliar, Papal, and Curial Texts* © 1982, ICEL; excerpts from the English translation of Book of Blessings © 1988, ICEL. All rights reserved.

Prayers from *Proclaiming Your Wonders* (Dominican Publications, 1991) are reprinted with the permission of Rev Nivard Kinsella OCSO.

'The Glory of These Forty Days' translated by M. F. Bell (1862–1947) from *The English Hymnal* is reprinted with the permission of Oxford University Press.

Excerpt from *Celebrations of the Word & Communion; For Sunday & Weekday Celebrations in the Absence of a Priest* © 1996, Liturgy Office, Bishops' Conference of England and Wales.